AF598973

American Sign Language

Weather

by E. Russell Primm III • illustrated by Kathleen Petelinsek

childsworld.com

Published by The Child's World®
800-599-READ • childsworld.com

Photography Credits
Olga_Kuzmina/Shutterstock.com, cover; FamVeld/Shutterstock.com, 1, 20; txking/Shutterstock.com, 3; MR.PRAWET THADTHIAM/Shutterstock.com, 4; Aleksandr Gogolin/Shutterstock.com, 5; A3pfamily/Shutterstock.com, 6; Pakhnyushchy/Shutterstock.com, 7; LedyX/Shutterstock.com, 8; Leonid Ikan/Shutterstock.com, 9; Minerva Studio/Shutterstock.com, 10; Triff/Shutterstock.com, 11; Afanasiev Andrii/Shutterstock.com, 12; prapann/Shutterstock.com, 13; Roxana Bashyrova/Shutterstock.com, 14; Serg64/Shutterstock.com, 15; Katrina Brown/Shutterstock.com, 16; Li Hui Chen/Shutterstock.com, 17; Yevhenii Chulovskyi/Shutterstock.com, 18; Subbotina Anna/Shutterstock.com, 19; JamesChen/Shutterstock.com, 21

ISBN Information
9781503889071 (Reinforced Library Binding)
9781503890152 (Portable Document Format)
9781503891395 (Online Multi-user eBook)
9781503892637 (Electronic Publication)

LCCN 2023950371

Printed in the United States of America

Note to Parents, Caregivers, and Educators: The understanding of any language begins with the acquisition of vocabulary, whether the language is spoken or manual. The books in this series provide readers, both young and old, with basic American Sign Language signs. Combining close photo cues and simple, but detailed, line illustrations, children and adults alike can begin the process of learning American Sign Language.

Let these books be an introduction to the world of American Sign Language. Most languages have regional dialects and multiple ways of expressing the same thought. This is also true for sign language. We have attempted to use the most common version of the signs for the words in this series. As with any language, the best way to learn is to be taught in person by a frequent user. It is our hope that this series will pique your interest in sign language.

A special thanks to our advisers: As a member of a deaf family that spans four generations, **Kim Bianco Majeri** lives, works, and plays among the Deaf community. **Carmine L. Vozzolo** is an educator of children who are deaf and hard of hearing, as well as their families.

E. Russell Primm III was a well-known figure in the publishing industry who produced thousands of acclaimed books for children. He was affiliated with organizations such as the American Library Association, the Chicago Book Clinic, and the University of Chicago Publishing Program Advisory Board.

Kathleen Petelinsek has loved books since she was a child. Through the years, she has written, designed, and illustrated many books for children. She lives in Wisconsin, near her granddaughter who also shares her love for books.

Predicting what the weather will be is called the forecast.

Weather

Make the "W" sign. Then make a zigzag motion and move your hand downward.

Thunder is caused by lightning heating the air.

Thunder

Tap your right ear with your index finger. Then move both fists right and left a few times.

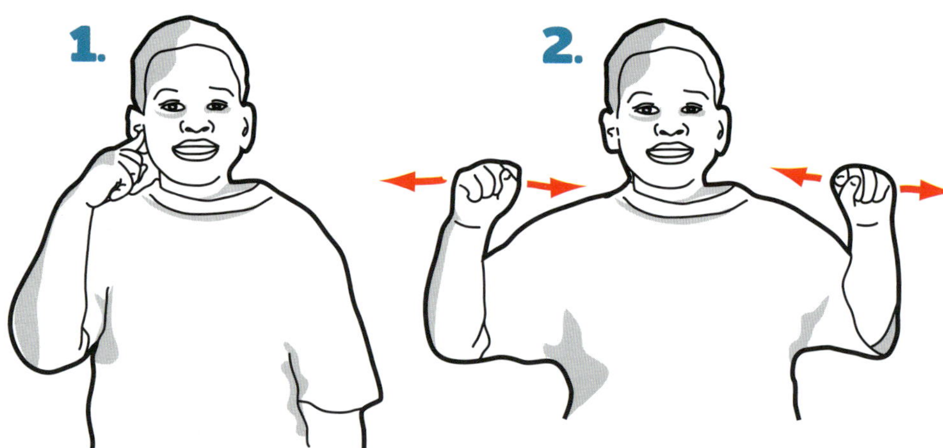

Lightning is made of electricity.

Lightning

Move your right index finger in a zigzag motion as it moves downward.

What do you like to do on a rainy day?

Rain

Slightly curve your hands and move them downward. Repeat.

The highest wind speed ever recorded was 253 miles per hour (407 km/h).

Wind

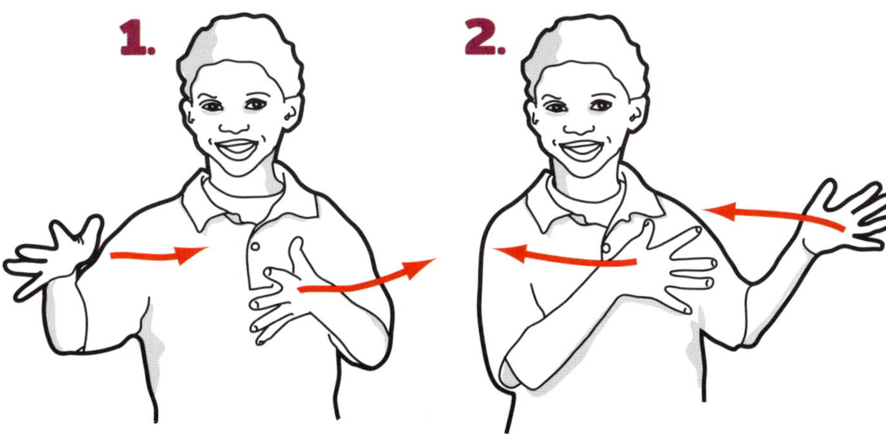

Open both hands (with palms facing each other) and move them from left to right. Repeat.

Snowflakes have six sides.

Snow

Wiggle all your fingers while moving your hands downward.

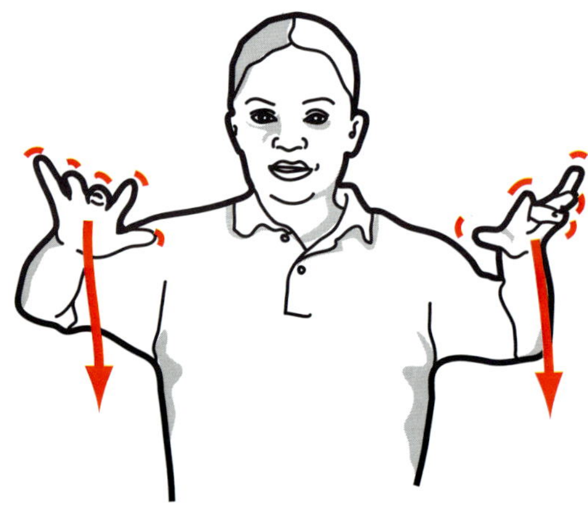

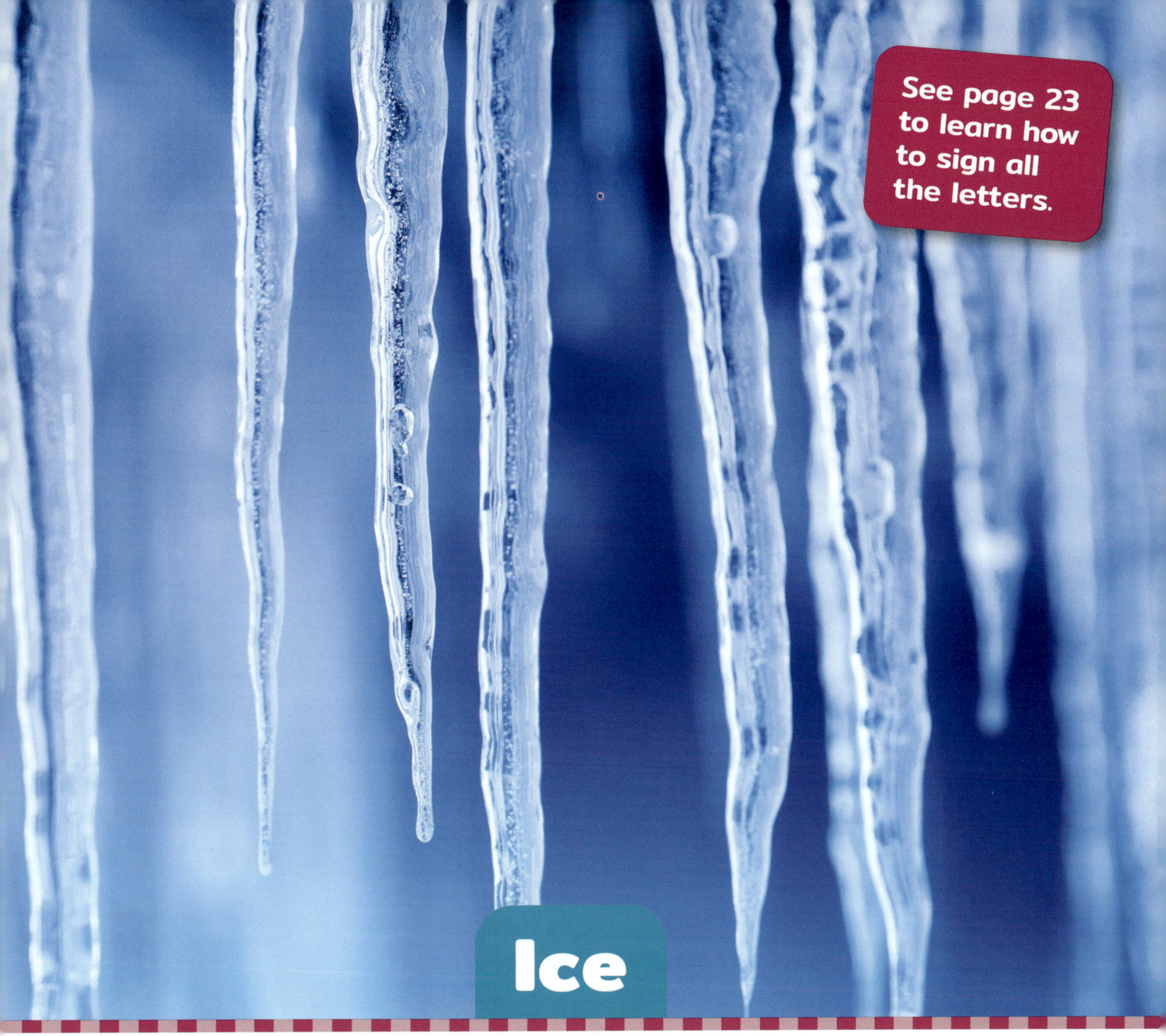

See page 23 to learn how to sign all the letters.

Ice

1.

2.

3.

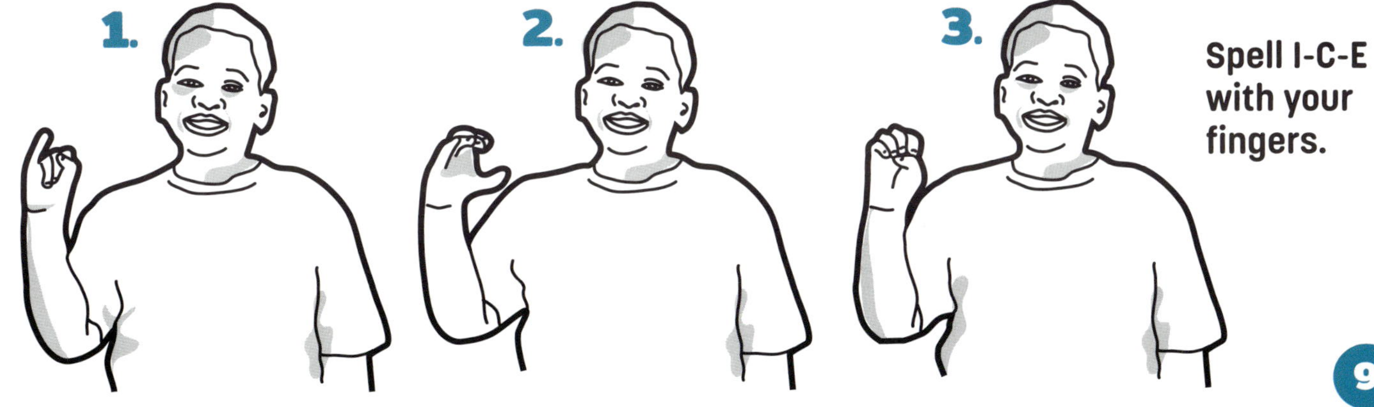

Spell I-C-E with your fingers.

Tornadoes usually occur in the spring and summer between the hours of 3 PM and 9 PM.

Tornado

Open both hands and bend your middle fingers inward. Move your arms so your two fingers revolve around each other—like a tornado.

Hurricanes are given a name to help scientists tell them apart.

Hurricane

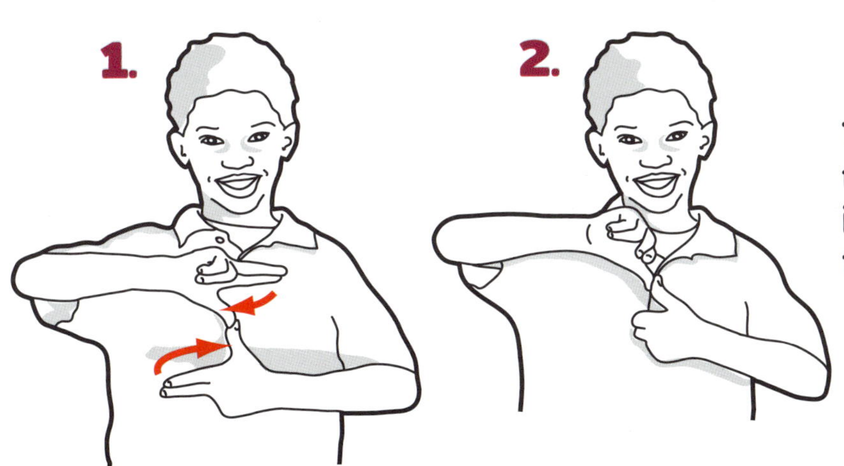

Touch your thumbs together. Bend both index and middle fingers over and over.

What colors do you see in the sky when the sun sets?

Sky

Spell S-K-Y with your fingers.

Clouds are made of tiny water droplets.

Cloud

Curl your fingers and face your palms toward each other. Move both hands in a spiral motion from left to right.

Like clouds, fog is also made up of tiny water droplets. Fog is much closer to the ground.

Fog

Spell F-O-G with your fingers.

Sunshine helps things grow and can make people feel happy.

Sunny

Touch your right thumb to your fingertips. Open your hand a little.

The hottest temperature ever recorded was 134.1°F (56.7°C) in Death Valley, California.

Hot

Curl your fingers toward your mouth. Move your hand down and away from your face.

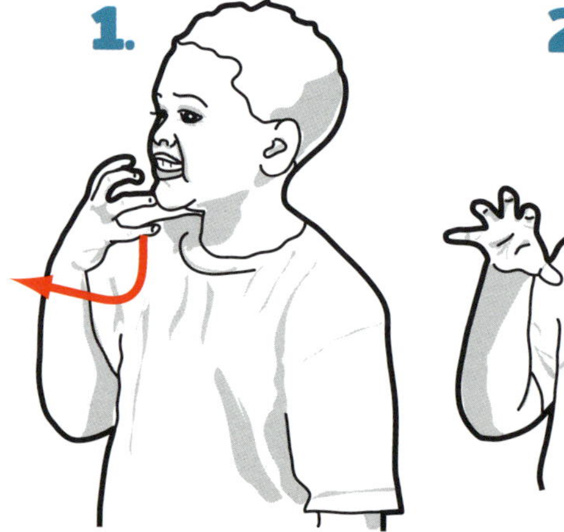

The coldest temperature ever recorded was −128.6°F (−89.2°C) in Antarctica.

Cold

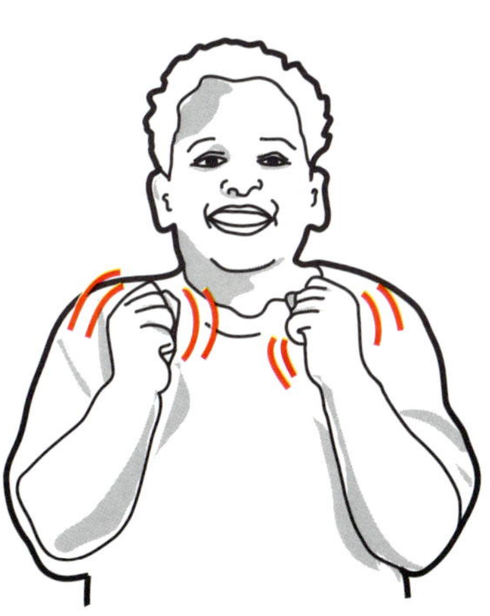

With both fists up, pretend to shiver.

Many animals hibernate during the winter.

Winter

Make the "W" sign and shiver as if you are cold.

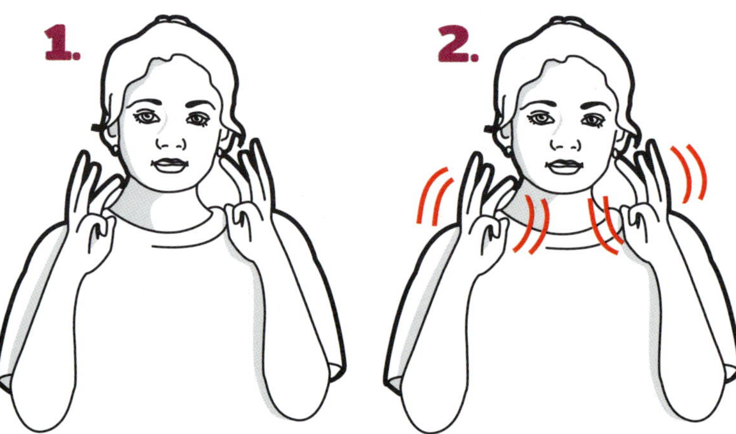

What is your favorite spring flower?

Spring

1.

2.

Put one hand around the other. Push up like a flower blooming.

What is your favorite summertime activity?

Summer

Move your right index finger from left to right across your forehead. Curl your finger when it reaches the right side.

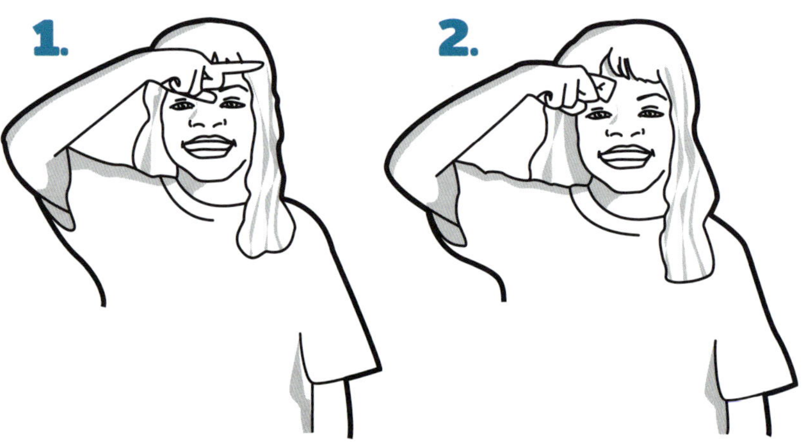

Farmers plant pumpkin seeds in early July to get a crop in the fall.

Fall

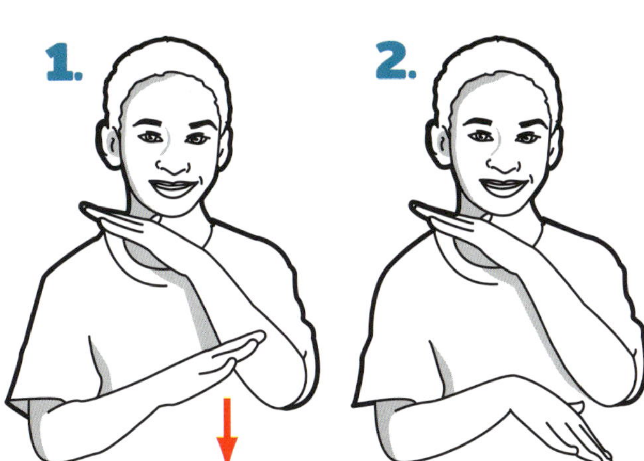

Hold your flat left arm like a tree. Wave your flat right arm like leaves falling from the tree.

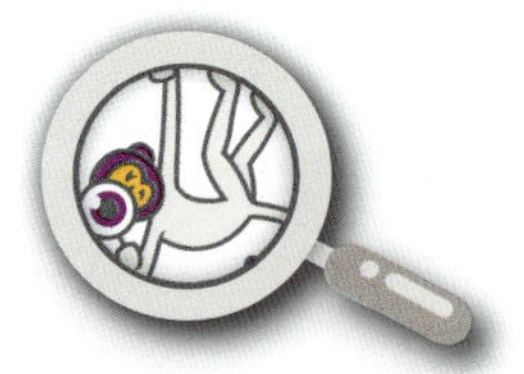

Wonder More

- How much did you know about American Sign Language (ASL) before reading this book? Do you already know some ASL signs? What new signs did you learn?

- Some words or specific names don't have signs. In these cases, you can spell the individual letters of the word, which is called fingerspelling. Look at the alphabet chart on page 23. Can you sign the letters in your name?

- With a partner, pick three signs from this book and practice them together. Are you able to understand each other? Is ASL easier or harder than you thought it would be?

- Did you know that your facial expression can affect the meaning of a sign? Why do you think our facial expressions are an important part of communication in ASL?

Sign Language Alphabet

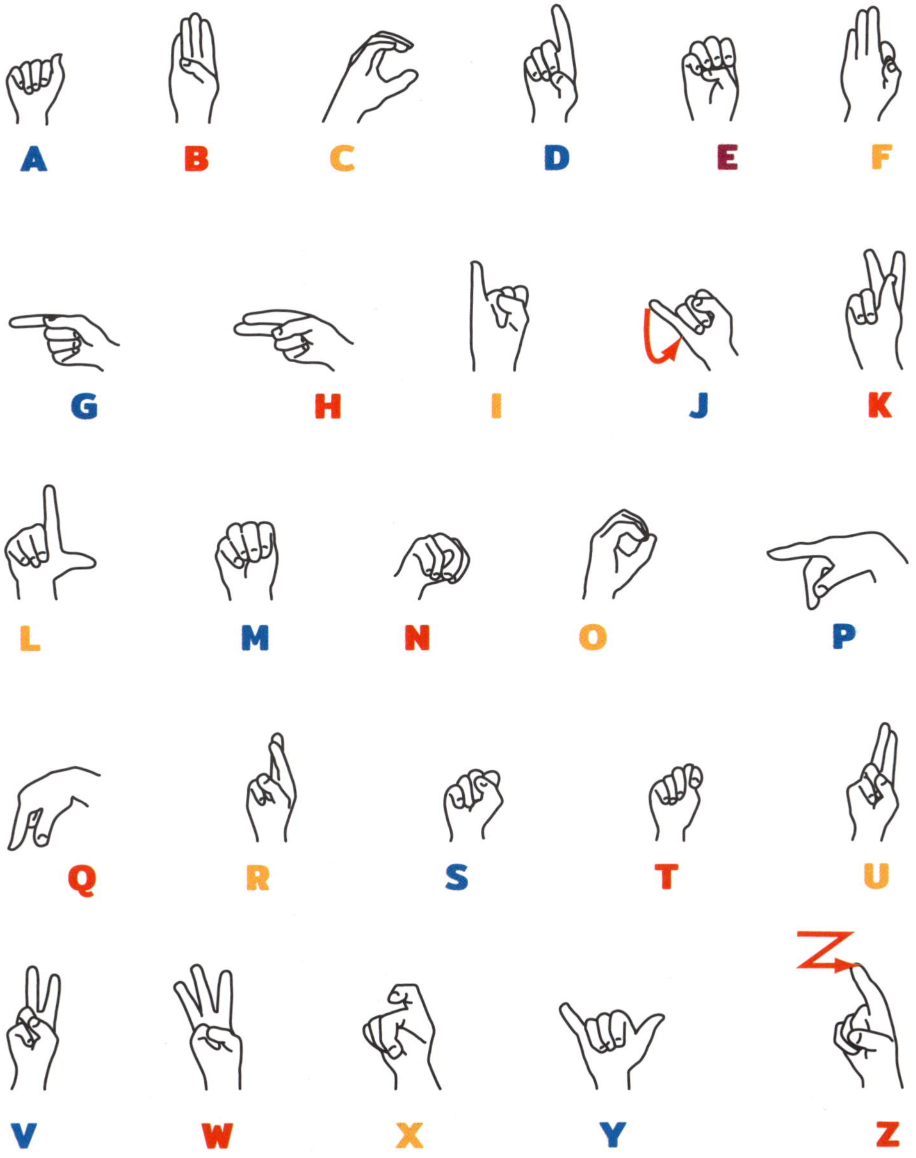

A B C D E F

G H I J K

L M N O P

Q R S T U

V W X Y Z

Find Out More

In the Library

Gallaudet University Press (editor). *The Gallaudet Children's Dictionary of American Sign Language*. Washington, DC: Gallaudet University Press, 2014.

MacLean, Roz. *More than Words: So Many Ways to Say What We Mean*. New York, NY: Henry Holt & Co., 2023.

On the Web

Visit our website for links about American Sign Language:
childsworld.com/links

Note to Parents, Caregivers, Teachers, and Librarians: We routinely verify our web links to make sure they are safe and active sites. So encourage your readers to check them out!

A Special Thank-You!

Thank you to our models from the Program for Children Who are Deaf and Hard of Hearing at the Alexander Graham Bell School in Chicago, Illinois.

Alina's favorite things to do are art, soccer, and swimming. DJ is her brother!

Aroosa is in third grade and loves reading, shopping, and playing with her sister, Aamna. Her favorite color is red.

Dareous likes football. His favorite team is the Detroit Lions. He also likes to play video games.

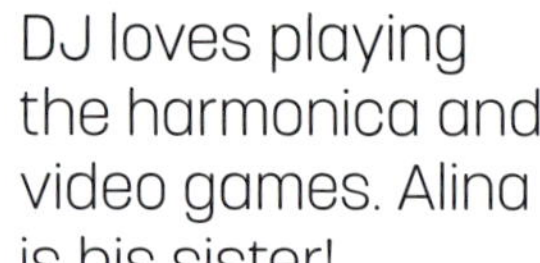

DJ loves playing the harmonica and video games. Alina is his sister!

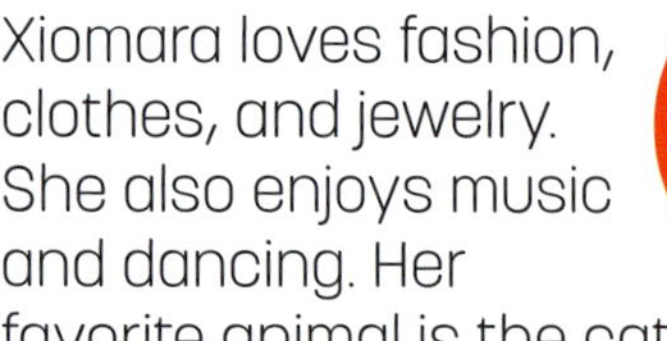

Xiomara loves fashion, clothes, and jewelry. She also enjoys music and dancing. Her favorite animal is the cat.